NATURE UNDERCOVER

NATURE UNDERCOVER

Hunters and Prey

Beatrice McLeod

Illustrations by Antonella Pastorelli, Paola Holguin, Ivan Stalio

Series Consultant:
Jim Kenagy, Ph.D., Professor of Zoology and Curator of Mammals, University of Washington

BLACKBIRCH PRESS, INC.
WOODBRIDGE, CONNECTICUT

Published in the United States in 2000
by Blackbirch Press, Inc.
260 Amity Road
Woodbridge, CT 06525
web site: http://www.blackbirch.com
e-mail: staff@blackbirch.com

Copyright © 2000 by McRae Books Srl, Florence (Italy)
First Edition

Hunters and Prey was created and produced by
McRae Books Srl, via de' Rustici, 5 – Florence (Italy)
e-mail: mcrae@tin.it

Text: Beatrice McLeod
Illustrations: Antonella Pastorelli, Paola Holguin, Andrea Ricciardi di Gaudesi, Ivan Stalio, Matteo Chesi
Picture research: Anne McRae
Graphic Design: Marco Nardi
Layout and cutouts: Adriano Nardi and Ornella Fassio
Color separations Litocolor, Florence

Printed in China

10 9 8 7 6 5 4 3 2 1

Library of Congress Cataloging-in-Publication Data
McLeod, Beatrice.
    Hunters and prey / by Beatrice McLeod.
    p. cm.
    Includes index.
    ISBN 1-56711-527-6
    1. Animals—Juvenile literature. 2. Predation (biology)—Juvenile literature. 3. Animal defenses—Juvenile literature.
[1. Animals—habits and behavior. 2. Animals—defenses.] I. Title II. Series
QL758M24 2000
591—dc21

Contents

Cassowary, page 14

Sea slug, page 11

Red-eyed tree frog, page 27

Viper, page 18

Net-throwing
spider, page 30

Polar bear, page 37

Introduction

All animals must eat to obtain the energy they need to survive. Many species—the carnivores—are active hunters that prey on live creatures to obtain their food. Other species—the herbivores—feed on plants. The hunters rely on a huge range of natural weapons and cunning strategies to capture their victims. The prey have developed just as many amazing ploys and defensive weapons to avoid detection and capture. This never-ending battle to outsmart each other may seem cruel to us, but, in the natural world, both predators and prey must fight for their survival. That is nature's way.

Puma, page 36

How this book works

Blending In
NOW YOU SEE ME, NOW YOU DON'T! Many animals use their body shape and color for camouflage—to blend into their surroundings. This enables them to move, eat, and rest with less chance of being spotted by predators. The leaf insects on this page (can you see them?) have even grown spots on their backs to mimic the mold on the leaves that surround them!

Each section in this book opens with a stunning, large-format illustration that shows hunters or prey in action or during a specific, typical moment in their lives. This leads into a two-page spread with many illustrations that show a range of animals from around the world and the strategies they employ to catch their next meal or to avoid being eaten.

Brief captions explain how each spot illustration relates to the subject.

Vivid, descriptive text accompanies a large illustration that provides a stunning, up-close view of nature in action.

A dynamic, full-color illustration introduces each section subject.

The introductory text gives an overview of the subject.

Detailed illustrations highlight specific adaptations.

Warning Signals

BRIGHT COLORS MEAN WATCH OUT! The poison-arrow frogs of Central and South America produce powerful poisons from special glands in their skins. They are among the most poisonous animals alive. In one species, just 0.0000003 of an ounce of their venom would be enough to kill a human adult! Many poison-arrow frogs advertise their deadly toxins with their brightly colored skins. Birds and other predators that normally feed on frogs learn that the garish colors on these amphibians mean "Stay away!"

The harmless **parrot snake** lives in the rain forests of Central America. It knows that by imitating the open-mouthed pose of more dangerous species—such as the viper—it will scare most predators away.

Racoons are quite at home in the trees. They often make their dens in hollow trunks. While resting on the top of an old tree trunk, a raccoon can keep an eye out and warn others of approaching danger.

Warning Signals

When danger is near, a warning signal like the brightly colored skin of the poison-arrow frog may be enough to discourage an attack. Most animals have one or more survival tricks or signals to use when a predator threatens. New World howler monkeys use their powerful, penetrating voices to scare away potential enemies. Certain herd animals use body movement to signal "Danger!" to others. Some animals rely on scary-looking spines, spikes, colors, or markings. Others imitate the behavior of dangerous species. Still others use foul odors to keep enemies at bay.

Porcupine fish are covered with spines that normally lie flat. When a predator approaches, the fish gulp down enough air or water to puff their bodies up, making the spines stick straight out. Their spiny, round shape makes them impossible to swallow.

When a predator looms near a herd of **springboks** on the treeless plains of southern Africa, the graceful antelopes make strange, twisted leaps into the air to warn other herd members of the approaching danger.

The piercing cries of **howler monkeys** can carry over distances of up to 3 miles (5 km). These primates live in territorial groups in the forests of Central and South America. Each group stakes out its territory with howling matches. Their loud, piercing cries mean "Keep out!"

The **Asian macaque** monkey uses body language to warn predators to keep their distance. This male is defending his troop by keeping his front legs wide apart so that he looks bigger than he is, and baring his full mouth of sharp teeth.

The **pronghorn** inhabits the plains and semi-arid deserts of North America. When danger threatens, pronghorns raise the elegant white ruffs on their rumps to warn others in the group before fleeing. Their long, slender legs make them extremely fast runners, reaching speeds of 53 miles per hour (85 km/h).

The South American **sun bittern** is very hard to see when it is sitting on its nest in the rain forest. Its mixed brown, gray, white, and olive plumage blends in well with the undergrowth. But if a predator stumbles upon its nest, the bird will try to startle it by spreading its wings and tail feathers, blinding the enemy with brilliant orange and brown feathers. The spots on the wings glare like a pair of eyes.

Brightly colored **sea slugs** have a very foul taste. Predators learn to associate the slug's brilliant colors with their dreadful taste and leave them alone.

The **thorny devil** is an Australian lizard— it's also one of the world's most bizzare reptiles. It is entirely covered in large and small spikes, which act as a warning to predators. Although it looks dangerous, the thorny devil is a gentle, harmless creature that feeds on ants.

Out of Harm's Way

SHARK ALARM! Seabirds, like this albatross, need quick reflexes in order to survive. As they float upon the water in the open ocean, they must beware of predators like the great white shark. The great white attacks rapidly and without warning. It uses the same hunting technique for seals, fish, seabirds, and any other prey: surprise attack. Without notice, a great white will pop out of the water, mouth open, ready to crunch prey. If its target is not able to react instantly, it will most likely become food for the ocean's fiercest predator.

Out of Harm's Way

Animals have many ways to escape or stay out of harm's way when predators threaten. Some, like the ostrich, use a simple burst of speed to outrun their attackers. Others roll themselves up into prickly balls or even dig themselves into the ground, where they are hard to see and difficult to get at. Turtles and tortoises have tough protective shells into which they withdraw their heads and other soft body parts.

When a predator grabs a **lizard** by its tail, it can break off so the reptile can run away. In just a short time, a new tail will grow back to replace the one that broke off.

Like all turtles and tortoises, this **Chinese yellow-margined box turtle** can completely close its shell in order to retreat from enemies. Just 6 inches (15 cm) long, it forages by day for plants and insects in both land and water habitats.

The **cassowary** is a large, flightless bird that lives in Australia and New Guinea. Armed with a dagger-like nail on one of its toes, it uses this weapon to strike out at predators. It also has a heavy, bony helmet, or casque, on the top of its head, which protects it from branches as it runs through the bush.

Flying squirrels are rodents that live in the forests of North America, Eurasia, and Africa. Despite their name, they don't actually fly. Instead, they glide using a special membrane of skin that is attached to the wrists of their forelimbs and the ankles of their hind legs. When danger looms, they can make long gliding leaps of up to 200 feet (60 m).

The **echidna**, or **spiny anteater** as this Australian egg-laying mammal is also known, escapes from danger by digging itself into the ground when threatened. When it is safe from attack, only its pointy spines are visible.

The **basilisk lizard** lives in the forests of Central America. It escapes by skittering across the surface of the water without sinking in. Basilisks have long, powerful back legs and broad feet with scaly, fringed toes, which allow them to actually "walk" on water.

The **giant clam** dwells inside a hard protective shell. When danger threatens, it clamps its shell together and stays safe inside.

Hedgehogs have more than 7,000 sharp spines covering their small bodies. When menaced, they curl themselves into a tight ball and protect their soft, vulnerable belly as much as possible. Their spines are also used to break a fall if they tumble off a ridge or bank.

Although **ostriches** have wings, these large birds are unable to fly. They are, however, among the fastest runners on Earth and can reach speeds of more than 45 mph (70 km/h).

Limpets are the favorite food of the **sunstar sea star**. To avoid being eaten, a limpet raises a slippery mantle up over its shell so that the sea star cannot grip it.

Sometimes keeping a low profile is the best way to avoid trouble. This **hare** crouches down amid the grass and keeps perfectly still in order to stay out of a predator's line of vision. If this doesn't work, the hare will leap up and dash away, relying on speed instead of stealth to escape the danger.

Natural Weapons

A DEADLY TONGUE. Chameleons are a group of lizards best known for their ability to change color. They prey on insects, scorpions, and spiders, although some of the larger species also feed on small mammals and birds. Chameleons have special adaptations to help them capture their prey. Their large eyes can swivel independently to locate prey or they can focus together to take aim. When a chameleon spots a victim, it flicks at it quickly with its tongue. Sticky patches on the tongue's end ensure that the prey cannot escape while it is being drawn back into the mouth. In this illustration, a three-horned Jackson's chameleon of southern Africa is striking at a migratory locust who has just taken its last flight!

Snakes in the **viper** family have a pair of hollow fangs in the upper jaw that they rotate forward to bite their victims. Once they bite, they inject venom through the fangs. It is usually only seconds until the animals die.

Scorpions have venomous stingers on the ends of their tails. They use these stingers to paralyze prey so that they can grasp and eat them with their pincerlike claws.

Natural Weapons

Many animals have one or more special "weapons" that they use to catch prey. Some, like vipers and scorpions, use venom to kill or paralyze their victims. Many birds have beaks with special adaptations that help them catch the food they like to eat. Large predators, including members of the cat family, are sleek, hunting machines—their whole bodies are adapted for pouncing in ambush.

Woodpeckers feed on insects that live under the bark of trees. They pick the insects out with their special chisel-shaped, heavy beaks.

Ant lion larvae—also called **doodlebugs**—dig themselves into funnel-shaped holes in the sand. When a victim approaches, they throw sand at it so that it stumbles into their waiting jaws.

Baleen whales have special material in their mouths to filter plankton and krill from the water.

After a **striped argiope spider** has spun a large, strong web, it sits and waits for prey. When an insect is trapped, it quickly wraps its victim in a silken ball.

An **octopus** uses its tentacles and suckers to grab prey. The sensitive tentacles are also used to strip the meat off victims and to carry the food to its mouth.

Like all cats, **bobcats** are superb hunters. Their supple bodies are adapted for creeping up on and pouncing on prey. Their sharp claws and teeth are used to catch and kill their victims.

Anteaters have extremely long, sticky tongues that they poke into ant and termite nests. The insects stick to the tongue, which the anteater then draws into its mouth.

Even though they have no eyes or ears, **sea stars** are excellent hunters. They use their senses of touch and smell to locate prey.

Skimmers or **scissorbills** skim the surface of lakes and rivers, snapping up fish with their specially shaped bills. The lower part of the bill is longer than the upper part— making it easier to catch fish.

The Antarctic **snowy sheatbill** uses the element of surprise to steal the krill a penguin mother is feeding to her chick.

Pythons and boas, like this **anaconda**, kill their prey by constriction and suffocation. Victims are wrapped in the snake's powerful coils and squeezed to death.

Scaring Predators Away

KEEPING DANGEROUS COMPANY. The plantlike creatures shown here are sea anemones. They sting and kill fish with rows of tiny poison-tipped "harpoons" on their tentacles. One species of fish—the anemone clownfish—is resistent to this poison. It swims happily among the dangerous tentacles. In return for a safe home and the food they scavenge from the anemones' leftover prey, the clownfish chase away the anemones' predators and keep their hosts clean.

Scaring Predators Away

Keeping predators away can be as simple as staying together in large groups. Some animals, like the clownfish, stay close to dangerous animals and use them as protection. In some cases, some animals may need to use direct action. This may involve making the first move—attacking predators when they come too close. Large animals, such as elephants, can do this very successfully. Smaller animals may have to bluff their attackers by puffing up their chests or feathers, or raising a ruff to look larger and more frightening than they really are.

The **praying mantis** usually uses camouflage for protection—blending into the background. When this fails, the insect will raise its arms and try to scare a predator away.

Stingrays are named for the long, sharp stingers in their tails. They use these stingers to defend themselves against attack.

Adult **musk oxen** keep their young safe by standing together in a circle with their horns facing outward. The calves stay hidden inside the circle.

When face to face with a predator, the **Virginia owl** puffs up its feathers and spreads its wings. This way, it looks bigger and more dangerous than it actually is. With its piercing eyes and sharp, open beak, it makes a menacing sight.

This diagram shows how adult musk oxen protect their calves. These animals live in arctic North America and Greenland where their only natural enemies are wolves.

When a predator gets too close, the **frilled lizard** of Australia raises the scaly membrane around its neck and opens it mouth in a threat display. This makes it look larger and more fearsome.

Tropical **jack fish** swarm together in a gyrating circle during the day to discourage barracudas and other fish from attacking them. They hunt by themselves at night under the cover of darkness.

Small birds will sometimes band together to attack a large predator. Here a **white wagtail** and a **yellow wagtail** are attacking a **cuckoo**. They are trying to keep the larger bird from taking over their nests and laying its eggs in them.

Even the most determined predator will think twice before attacking the Australian **blue-tongued lizard** when it suddenly flashes its large, brightly colored tongue.

Many animals, including the **cobra**, have "eye spots" on their bodies. These false eyes make predators think that they are being watched even when their prey is looking in the other direction.

The **African elephant** spreads its ears, lowers its head, and charges furiously at any predator that dares to threaten its young. In this mood, it will trample underfoot anything in its way. Even groups of lions quickly retreat when charged.

Blending In

NOW YOU SEE ME, NOW YOU DON'T! Many animals use their body shape and color for camouflage—to blend into their surroundings. This enables them to move, eat, and rest with less chance of being spotted by predators. The leaf insects on this page (can you see them?) have even grown spots on their backs to mimic the mold on the leaves that surround them!

The **mantis** mimics the colors of surrounding twigs and stays so still that predators can't see it.

The brightly colored **rainbow lorikeet** may hang upside down to make itself appear more like the surrounding green vegetation of its habitat.

Blending In

The most effective way to avoid predators is not to be seen by them. An evolutionary process called "natural selection," which takes thousands of years, helps living things adapt in order to survive. This process has enabled leaf insects and many animals achieve body shapes and colors that make them difficult to see in their natural environments. Individuals that are less easily spotted by predators are more likely to survive and to pass their successful characteristics on to their offspring.

Hairy frogfish lie motionless on the seafloor. Their plantlike bodies look like algae-covered rocks. This disguise not only keeps them safe from predators, but also makes them invisible to unsuspecting prey, which the frogfish swallows when the prey drifts within reach.

This Brazilian **potoo**'s feathers are exactly the same color as the old tree trunk on which it is perching. To make itself even harder to see, it keeps perfectly still with its head held high. This way, it looks just like the top of the trunk.

The little **cockatoo waspfish** resembles dead sea grass. It normally stays near the seafloor and rolls gently with the natural flow of the water. If a predator comes close, the fish raises its row of venomous spines along its dorsal fin.

The **red-eyed tree frog** lives in the rain forests of Central America. Its bright colors are similar to those of the colorful plants that grow in its lush habitat.

The Arctic **white-tailed ptarmigan** has a coat for every season. In summer (above), its speckled plumage blends with the tundra. In autumn (right), it begins to molt and new white feathers appear. This is perfect camouflage for a habitat mixed with snow and rock. In winter (below) the ptarmigan grows a full coat of thick, white feathers that make it nearly invisible in a snowy landscape.

Zebras live in herds on the African savannas. In groups, their striped coats confuse predators and make individuals hard to see.

In the shimmering heat and dust of the African grasslands, **ostriches** fluff up their tail feathers. From a distance they look like a clump of bushes,

A **lioness**'s tawny coat blends with the dry grass of the African plain. This keeps her safe while resting and allows her to sneak up on prey.

Special Abilities

NATURAL SONAR. Bats hunt at night using a sophisticated system of sound navigation called echolocation. As they fly through the darkness, they send out a series of high-pitched cries. Their sensitive hearing picks up the echoes that bounce back at them off their surroundings. Echolocation enables bats to locate even tiny insects and to hunt in total darkness. Here, two hognosed bats pursue a moth in the pitch-black night.

Mongooses love to eat birds' eggs. Their routine consists of picking up an egg, licking it, throwing it back between their legs against a rock, and then eating the white and the yolk from the ground.

Electric rays feed on fishes that they capture by stunning them with electric shocks. These rays have large electric organs along their body axis that can emit shocks of over 300 volts.

Most spiders spin webs and then wait for prey to get caught in them. But the **net-throwing spider** spins her web and holds it in her back legs. She waits for prey to pass underneath and then throws her net over them.

This species of **Darwin's finch** is one of just a handful of animals that use "tools" to hunt. These birds choose twigs or thorns and use them to poke prey out from under tree bark.

Special Abilities

Some animals—such as bats that can echolocate—have amazing physical adaptations that make them expert hunters. Other special abilities include great speed, electric shocks that stun victims, and excellent eyesight or hearing. A few species have developed special behaviors, including the use of simple tools, to capture prey. Among the primates—the group that includes our closest relatives—native intelligence and memory have made them very effective hunters.

The **archer fish** can shoot spurts of water at insects on vegetation that overhangs the water. This knocks the prey into the water where they can be eaten.

Egg-eater snakes can unhinge their jaws and stretch their mouths wide open to swallow large eggs. They also have bones in their throats that can pierce the eggs and draw out the insides.

Peregrine falcons are among the fastest animals on Earth. They fly high and dive at speeds of up to 175 mph (280 km/h), striking with clenched claws that kill their prey on impact.

All birds of prey have excellent eyesight. They use this sense to locate prey from a distance. The **great gray owl** is no exception, but it also uses its very acute hearing to focus in on its prey's location.

The **black heron** wades through the water, with one or both wings raised to cast a shadow on the surface. This blocks out the sun's glare, enabling it to see better below the surface. It also creates a false sense of security for the fish below, who feel safer in shaded areas.

This baby **baboon** has discovered a new food source and is stealing an ostrich egg. Mammals in general are capable of flexible behavior, exploration, and learning.

The **jacana** is also known as a "lily trotter" for its peculiar ability to walk across water lily pads as it feeds on insects, fish, and seeds. It has very long toes and claws, which spread its weight over a large area of the pads. This prevents the bird from sinking.

Group Strength

PACK ATTACK! Gray wolves of the far north live together in packs. They eat a wide range of food, although moose, deer, and caribou are the prey they like best. Killing an animal ten times their size requires cooperation. Wolf packs normally trail a herd and pick out an old, young, or injured animal. Working together, they separate an individual from the herd before they attack. These wolves followed this old moose during the night, attacking it continuously and then backing off as it fought back. Now exhausted, the moose will soon surrender to the relentless attack of the pack.

Group Strength

Animals that hunt in packs or teams have many advantages. Cooperation allows groups of smaller animals to bring down much larger prey. This strategy also increases the range of food available to small predators. Working as a team, animals can also drive small prey, such as fish, into dense groups, which makes them easier to catch. When the prey has been caught, members of the group keep watch and drive away other predators who may want to steal their food.

Great white pelicans work as a team to catch fish. Groups of up to 500 individuals gather in V-shaped formations to herd schools of fish along in front of them. When the schools are dense enough, the pelicans dip their heads into the water, and scoop the fish up in their large bills.

African wild dogs work as a pack to hunt down prey. The dogs have enormous stamina and will chase after a victim for hours. Once the prey is exhausted, the dogs close in for the kill. These dogs have cornered a warthog and are using teamwork to make sure it doesn't escape.

The rare **giant otter** inhabits the slow-flowing rivers of South America. Unlike other otters, this species uses team tactics to hunt. They dive in unison to catch fish and work together to bring down large prey, including South American crocodiles, called caymans.

Blue-footed boobies fly together in flocks over the sea. When they locate a school of fish, they circle above it. Then, in response to initial calls by a few birds, they all dive at the same time. They hit the water at around 60 mph (100 km/h). Their dive carries them several feet into the water, where they snap up fish in their beaks.

Blowing bubbles through their airholes, a group of **humpback whales** creates a spiral "net" around a school of herrings (1). The bubble net forces the herrings toward the surface (2), where they are easy prey for the whales.

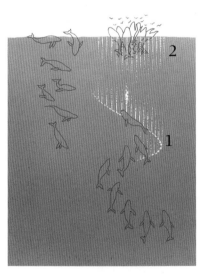

Among **lions**, females work together to do most of the hunting. One female will hide in the grass while the others drive prey toward her. The victim is usually too panicked to recognize the trap until it is too late.

Like many members of the dog family, **jackals** use team tactics to hunt. When their prey has been caught, however, fights will sometimes break out between group members over who will eat first.

In the deserts of western North America, the agile **roadrunner** uses its speed to catch insects, lizards, and rattlesnakes. It can fly, but does most of its hunting on the ground. It uses its long tail and wings for balance while running.

North America's largest cat, the **puma** (also known as the **mountain lion** or **cougar**), lives and hunts alone. When the ranges of two pumas overlap, the animals are careful to avoid each other. Each will mark its territory with droppings, urine, scent, and scratch marks.

Lone Hunters

Cooperation or pack hunting works for wolves, lions, boobies, and many others, but some animals prefer to hunt alone. The lone hunters tend to be large and powerful, or they possess special weapons for killing. North America's largest bears—the grizzly and polar—are massive animals with enormous strength. Big cats—pumas, leopards, and caracals—have great agility and speed. Birds of prey, like eagles, are equipped with keen eyesight, hooked beaks, and long, sharp talons for gripping and ripping apart their prey.

The huge **grizzly** or **brown bear** of northern North America and Eurasia weighs up to 1,000 lbs. (450 kg) and can charge at up to 31 mph (50 km/h). These huge animals feed mainly on plants and berries, but may include some small animals in their diet. When salmon run the rivers to spawn (lay eggs), the usually solitary bears line the banks. They lie in wait for the succulent fish, whipping them out with their paws.

The **white-bellied sea eagle** circles above the ocean, using its sharp eyesight to pinpoint fish beneath the waves. It dives down with its daggerlike talons outstretched and digs into its prey. This usually kills the victim on impact.

The solitary **aardvark** feeds almost exclusively on ants and termites. Its long toes are equipped with sharp claws that rip open insect nests. Its 12-inch- (30-cm) long sticky tongue laps up its victims.

At the sight of a fish in the water, the **kingfisher** takes aim. It plunges off its perch, wings flattened against its sides for extra speed. Once it hits the water, it grabs the fish and returns to its perch where it kills the prey by banging it against a hard object.

The **caracal**'s finely tuned hearing is helped by the fact that it can swivel its ears in any direction without moving its head. This enables the cat to hear prey anywhere.

The **nightjar** hunts for insects at dusk and dawn. As it flies, it holds its beak, which is surrounded by sensitive bristles, wide open. Even in darkness, the nightjar can feel the insects near its mouth and knows when to snap its beak shut on a victim.

Polar bears live in the Arctic where their thick, shaggy coats protect them from the cold. The solitary bears are patient hunters. When they find a seal's breathing hole in the ice, they crouch over it for hours, waiting for the seals to come up for air. Then they snatch the seals with their long claws.

Some lone hunters mark their territory using scents. This **leopard** is spraying a tree with urine containing a chemical scent produced by a special gland under its tail. This tells other leopards to "Keep away."

For More Information

Books

Collard, Sneed. *Tough Terminators: Twelve of the Earth's Most Fascinating Predators.* Minocqua, WI: NorthWord Press, 1994.

Kops, Deborah. *Falcons* (Wild Birds of Prey). Woodbridge, CT: Blackbirch Press, Inc., 2000.

Mullin, Rita, Carolyn Mitchell. *Who's For Dinner? Predators and Prey* (Animal Planet). New York, NY: Crown Publishing, 1998.

Swan, Erin. *Land Predators of North America* (Animals in Order). Danbury, CT: Franklin Watts, 1999.

Web Site

The Art of Camouflage

www.arts.ufl.edu/art/rt_room/sparkers/camuoflage/camouflage.html

Explanation of how and why animals use camouflage, and an art project to create your own animal camouflage.

Index